LOOK
& LEARN
farm
animals

LOOK
& LEARN

farm
animals

a first point & say book

HERMES
HOUSE

Cow

Cows live in a cowshed.

Cows live together in big groups called herds.

Calf

A baby cow is called a calf.

Calves drink their mother's milk.

Cows look after their calves in the cowshed.

Horse

Many horses live on farms.

Horses eat grass.

Some horses sleep in a warm stable at night.

A horse can see over the stable door.

Inside the stable there is food and water for the horse.

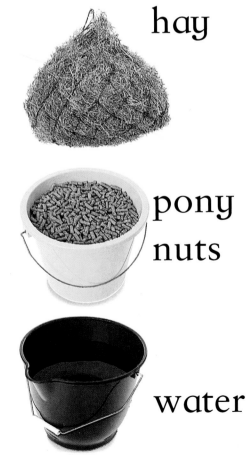

hay

pony nuts

water

Foal

A baby horse is called a foal.

Foals can stand up as soon as they are born.

Foals eat grass with their mothers.

Foals live in the stable too.

Look at my long, thin legs!

Foals like to play.

Pig

Pigs root around in the ground to find things to eat.

Mother pigs have little pink piglets.

Piglet

A baby pig is called a piglet.

Piglets have curly tails.

Piglets live in a sty.

Piglets have lots of brothers and sisters.

Sheep

Sheep have long, woolly coats. Sheep like to eat hay.

Sheep live in big groups called flocks.

A baby sheep is called a lamb. Little lambs nuzzle close to their mothers to keep warm and safe.

Sheep live in fields.

Goat

Goats have long beards.

They live in fields.

Kid

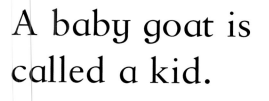

A baby goat is called a kid.

Kids stay close to their mother.

Duckling

Baby ducks
are called
ducklings.

Ducklings
like to play
with their
mothers.

Ducklings
live in a nest.

Soon it is
time for their
first swim.

Ducks have
special feet
for swimming.

Chick

A baby chicken
is called a chick.

Chicks
hatch
out of
eggs.

Chicks
are fluffy.

They soon
grow feathers.

Dog

A dog helps the shepherd bring the sheep home.

Baby dogs are
called puppies.
They learn
how to help
on the farm.

Most dogs are
kept as pets.

Do you know a
friendly dog?

Bees

Honeybees collect pollen from flowers.

These bees are kept in wooden boxes called hives.

Thousands of bees live in the hive.

The beekeeper wears special clothes.

Bees make honey inside the hive.

honeycomb

Honey is good to eat.

Can you match the right name

dog

sheep

cat

chicken

goat

horse

pig

duck

to the right animal?

This edition is published by Hermes House

Hermes House is an imprint of Anness Publishing Ltd
Hermes House, 88-89 Blackfriars Road, London SE1 8HA
tel. 020 7401 2077; fax 020 7633 9499; info@anness.com

1 3 5 7 9 10 8 6 4 2

Publisher: Joanna Lorenz
Designer: Julie Francis
Senior Editor: Catherine Barry

Picture Credits:
Bruce Coleman, Ecoscene, Holt Studios, FLPA, Nature Photographers, Papillio Photographic,
Planet Earth Pictures, Tony Stone, Warren Photographic/Jane Burton, Zefa Pictures

Previously published as part of a larger compendium, *Point and Say: Animal Friends*

1 3 5 7 9 10 8 6 4 2